How to Use this Book

Matched to the National Curriculum, this Collins Year 2 Reading Comprehension workbook is designed to improve comprehension skills.

Diverse and engaging texts including **fiction**, **non-fiction** and **poetry**.

Tests **increase in difficulty** as you work through the book.

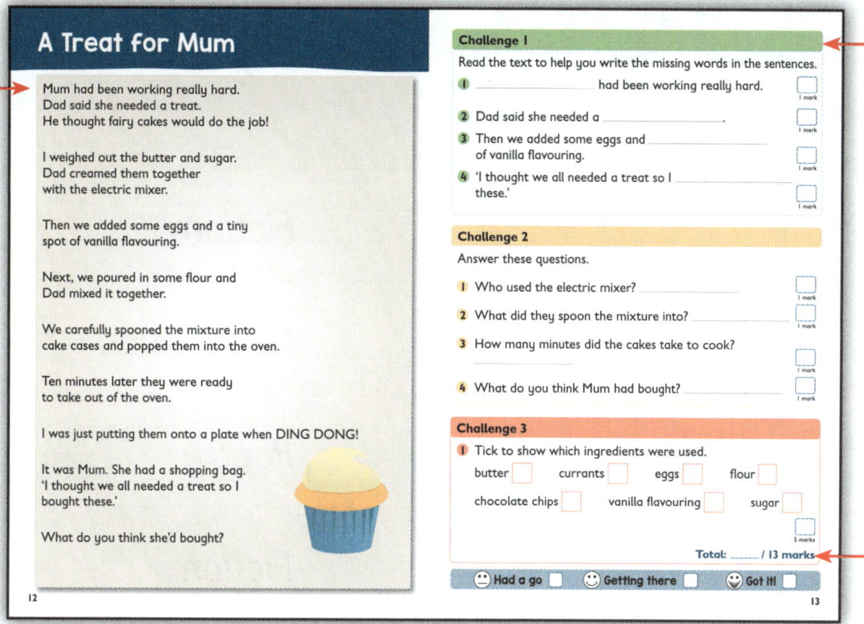

Questions split into three levels of difficulty – **Challenge 1**, **Challenge 2** and **Challenge 3** – to help progression.

Total marks boxes for recording progress and '**How am I doing**' checks for self-evaluation.

Starter test recaps skills covered in Year 1.

Three **Progress tests** included throughout the book for ongoing assessment and monitoring progress.

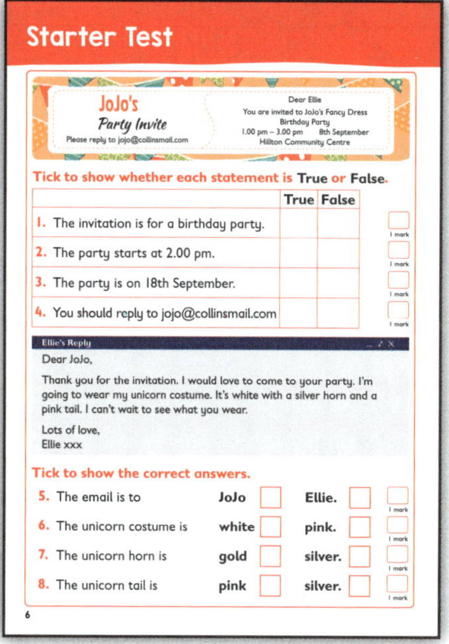

Answers are included at the back of the book.

Author: Rachel Clarke

Contents

Acknowledgments

The author and publisher are grateful to the copyright holders for permission to use quoted materials and images.

All illustrations and images are © Shutterstock.com and © HarperCollins*Publishers* Ltd.

Published by Collins
An imprint of HarperCollins*Publishers*
1 London Bridge Street
London SE1 9GF

HarperCollins*Publishers*
Macken House, 39/40 Mayor Street Upper,
Dublin 1, D01 C9W8, Ireland

© HarperCollins*Publishers* Limited 2025

ISBN 978-0-00-846756-2

First published 2021

This edition published 2025

10 9

Without limiting the exclusive rights of any author, contributor or the publisher of this publication, any unauthorised use of this publication to train generative artificial intelligence (AI) technologies is expressly prohibited. HarperCollins also exercise their rights under Article 4(3) of the Digital Single Market Directive 2019/790 and expressly reserve this publication from the text and data mining exception.

British Library Cataloguing in Publication Data.

A CIP record of this book is available from the British Library.

Publisher: Fiona McGlade
Author: Rachel Clarke
Copyeditor: Fiona Watson
Project Management: Shelley Teasdale
Cover Design: Sarah Duxbury
Inside Concept Design and Page Layout: Ian Wrigley
Production: Karen Nulty
Printed in the UK by Martins the Printers

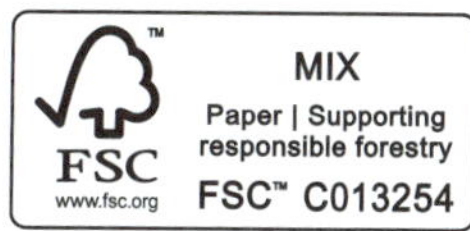

Reading Comprehension at Home

These ideas for games and activities can be easily carried out at home when reading for pleasure with your child, or when your child is reading for pleasure on their own. They will help build your child's comprehension skills and are fun to do.

Sing nursery rhymes

Nursery rhymes are a good way for children to learn about rhythm, rhyme and pattern. Lots of nursery rhymes are mini stories with beginnings, middles and ends, and different characters and settings, just like longer stories. Nursery rhymes also introduce children to older and more unusual words that they might otherwise not come across.

Share wordless picture books

Wordless picture books are excellent for encouraging children to tell their own stories based on the illustrations. Take turns with your child to tell a story using a wordless picture book. It's good fun to use character voices and to change the way you read (quickly, slowly, quietly, loudly, etc.) to reflect the meaning in the illustrations.

Make puppets

Making puppets to help retell a story is great fun too. You can make puppets from clothes pegs, wooden spoons, old socks and pieces of card stuck to lollipop sticks. Retelling a story in this way helps your child remember the sequence of events and to begin to think about the thoughts and feelings of different characters.

Read aloud

Reading aloud is one of the best ways to encourage your child to develop a love of reading. Try to make time to read aloud to your child every day. This can be from a storybook, a poem or an information book. Make the reading as pleasurable as you can, maybe by sharing a drink or treat together, or by cuddling up as you read.

Make connections

When you are reading with your child, encourage them to make connections between the book and their own experiences. For example, you may want to ask them if they remember a time when they had a similar experience to a character in the book; if they can think of other poems with similar characters, settings or themes; or if they've seen or heard about the information you read in a non-fiction book.

What happens next?

When you are reading a story or narrative poem with your child, stop at a suitable point in the story and ask them to predict what they think will happen next, and why. Encourage them to think about how their understanding of the characters and the events so far helped them with their prediction.

Word families

When you are reading with your child, take the time to explore the meaning of unfamiliar words, to ensure they understand what they have read. Encourage them to use the context to help them to work out what new words mean, but don't be afraid to use a dictionary to check the meaning. Collect words your child is familiar with and which have similar meanings to develop their understanding.

Picture perfect

When you are reading non-fiction with your child, consider the pictures and diagrams that have been included, as well as the words. Discuss why those particular pictures or diagrams might have been chosen, and how they help the reader to understand the text. Ask your child to suggest other pictures and diagrams they would like to see included on the page.

Join the library

Borrowing books from your local library is an easy and inexpensive way to ensure that your child experiences a wide range of books. Children's librarians are experts at ensuring their collections are full of well-loved classics, new releases, comics, audio stories and interesting non-fiction. Many local libraries also run story sessions and arrange activity sessions aimed at encouraging reading.

Starter Test

<table>
<tr><td colspan="2">

JoJo's
Party Invite

Please reply to jojo@collinsmail.com

</td><td>

Dear Ellie
You are invited to JoJo's Fancy Dress
Birthday Party
1.00 pm – 3.00 pm   8th September
Hillton Community Centre

</td></tr>
</table>

Tick to show whether each statement is True or False.

		True	False	
1.	The invitation is for a birthday party.			I mark
2.	The party starts at 2.00 pm.			I mark
3.	The party is on 18th September.			I mark
4.	You should reply to jojo@collinsmail.com			I mark

Ellie's Reply _ ↗ ✕

Dear JoJo,

Thank you for the invitation. I would love to come to your party. I'm going to wear my unicorn costume. It's white with a silver horn and a pink tail. I can't wait to see what you wear.

Lots of love,
Ellie xxx

Tick to show the correct answers.

5. The email is to **JoJo** ☐ **Ellie.** ☐   I mark

6. The unicorn costume is **white** ☐ **pink.** ☐   I mark

7. The unicorn horn is **gold** ☐ **silver.** ☐   I mark

8. The unicorn tail is **pink** ☐ **silver.** ☐   I mark

One, Two, Three, Four, Five

One, two, three, four, five,
Once I caught a fish alive.
Six, seven, eight, nine, ten.
Then I let it go again.

Why did I let it go?
Because it bit my finger so!
Which finger did it bite?
This little finger on my right!

Draw lines to match the rhyming words.

9. five   so

I mark

10. ten   right

I mark

11. go   alive

I mark

12. bite   again

I mark

Answer these questions.

13. What is the title of the poem?

I mark

14. How many lines does the poem have?

I mark

15. What type of animal is the poem about?

I mark

Sing a Song of Sixpence

Sing a song of sixpence, a pocket full of rye,

Four and twenty blackbirds baked in a pie.

When the pie was opened, the birds began to sing,

Oh wasn't that a dainty dish to set before the king?

The king was in his counting house, counting out his money,

The queen was in the parlour, eating bread and honey

The maid was in the garden, hanging out the clothes,

When down came a blackbird and pecked off her nose!

Read the poem to help you write the missing words in the sentences.

16. Sing a song of sixpence, a ______________ full of rye,

1 mark

17. Four and twenty blackbirds ______________ in a pie.

1 mark

18. When the pie was opened, the birds began
to ______________,

1 mark

19. Oh wasn't that a dainty ______________ to set
before the king?

1 mark

20. The king was in his counting house, ______________
out his money,

1 mark

21. The queen was in the parlour, ______________
bread and honey

1 mark

22. The maid was in the ________________, hanging out the clothes,

1 mark

23. When down came a blackbird and ________________ off her nose!

1 mark

Answer these questions about the poem.

24. How many blackbirds were baked in the pie?

____

1 mark

25. What happened when the pie was opened?

____

1 mark

26. Who was counting out their money? ________________

1 mark

27. Where was the queen? ________________

1 mark

28. What was the maid doing in the garden? ________________

____

1 mark

Draw lines to match the rhyming words.

29. rye   honey

1 mark

30. sing   pie

1 mark

31. money   nose

1 mark

32. clothes   king

1 mark

Banana Milkshake

You will need:

- 100g ice
- 2 medium bananas
- 200ml milk

- An electric blender
- 2 large glasses
- An adult to help you

What to do:

- Crush the ice in the blender.
- Peel and slice the bananas.
- Add the bananas and the milk to the crushed ice.
- Blend until the mixture is smooth.
- Pour the mixture into the glasses.

Now drink and enjoy your banana milkshake.

33. Tick to show which ingredients you need to make a banana milkshake.

butter ☐ bananas ☐ ice ☐

milk ☐ icing sugar ☐ flour ☐

3 marks

Read the recipe and circle the correct answers.

34. Crush the ice in the **glasses** **blender.**

1 mark

35. Peel and slice the **bananas** **milk.**

1 mark

36. Blend until the mixture is **lumpy** **smooth.**

1 mark

37. Pour the mixture into the **crushed ice glasses.**

1 mark

A Trip to the Zoo

Mum woke Polly and Peter up early. It was Saturday and it was time to go to the zoo. They got into the car and drove for an hour.

First, they went to see the monkeys. Polly thought they were funny as they swung through the trees.

Then they went to see the lions. They were all fast asleep.

Next, they went to the picnic area. They ate sandwiches and crisps.

After lunch, they went to the aquarium to see the penguins. Peter loved the way they waddled about on their short legs.

There was just time to visit the gift shop before going home.

Write the missing words in the sentences.

38. Mum woke Polly and Peter up ______________.

I mark

39. They got into the ______________ and drove for an hour.

I mark

40. First, they went to see the ______________.

I mark

Circle the correct answers.

41. Polly and Peter went to the zoo on **Saturday Sunday**.

I mark

42. It took them **two hours**   **an hour** to get there.

I mark

43. The lions were **asleep**   **eating**.

I mark

Total: ______ / 45 marks

A Treat for Mum

Mum had been working really hard.
Dad said she needed a treat.
He thought fairy cakes would do the job!

I weighed out the butter and sugar.
Dad creamed them together
with the electric mixer.

Then we added some eggs and a tiny
spot of vanilla flavouring.

Next, we poured in some flour and
Dad mixed it together.

We carefully spooned the mixture into
cake cases and popped them into the oven.

Ten minutes later they were ready
to take out of the oven.

I was just putting them onto a plate when DING DONG!

It was Mum. She had a shopping bag.
'I thought we all needed a treat so I
bought these.'

What do you think she'd bought?

Read the text to help you write the missing words in the sentences.

1 ______________________________ had been working really hard.

1 mark

2 Dad said she needed a ______________________________ .

1 mark

3 Then we added some eggs and ______________________________ of vanilla flavouring.

1 mark

4 'I thought we all needed a treat so I ______________________________ these.'

1 mark

Challenge 2

Answer these questions.

1 Who used the electric mixer? ______________________________

1 mark

2 What did they spoon the mixture into? ______________________________

1 mark

3 How many minutes did the cakes take to cook?

____

1 mark

4 What do you think Mum had bought? ______________________________

1 mark

Challenge 3

1 Tick to show which ingredients were used.

butter ☐   currants ☐   eggs ☐   flour ☐

chocolate chips ☐   vanilla flavouring ☐   sugar ☐

5 marks

Total: ______ / 13 marks

😐 **Had a go** ☐   🙂 **Getting there** ☐   😃 **Got it!** ☐

Honey Bees

Honey bees live in groups called **colonies**. Some colonies live in **hives**. Inside the hive there is a **queen bee**. There are also female bees called **worker bees** and male bees called **drones**.

The queen bee's job is to lay eggs.
The worker bees' job is to collect **pollen** and **nectar** from flowers.

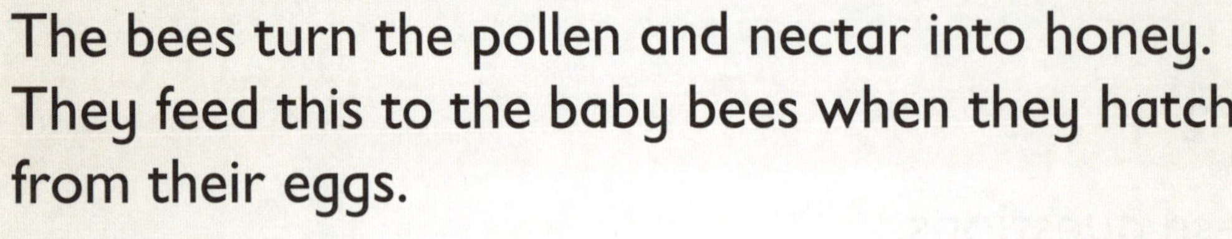

The bees turn the pollen and nectar into honey. They feed this to the baby bees when they hatch from their eggs.

Luckily for us, honey bees make more honey than they need. **Beekeepers** collect the honey from beehives for us to eat. They wear special suits to protect them from the bees' stings.

Beekeepers pour the honey into jars so it is ready for us to eat.

Glossary

beekeepers – people who keep bees

colonies – a group of bees that live together

drones – male bees

hives – the house or box that bees are kept in

nectar – a sugary liquid made by plants

pollen – dusty powder made by plants

queen bee – the bee in a colony that lays eggs

worker bees – female bees

Read the text to help you write the missing words in the sentences.

1 Honey bees live in ________________ called colonies. _I mark_

2 Inside the ________________ there is a queen bee. _I mark_

3 Beekeepers ________________ the honey into jars. _I mark_

Tick to show whether each statement is **True** or **False**.

	True	False	
1 Honey bees live in colonies.			_I mark_
2 Drones lay eggs in the hive.			_I mark_
3 Worker bees collect honey from flowers.			_I mark_
4 Beekeepers collect pollen from hives for us to eat.			_I mark_
5 Beekeepers wear special suits to protect them from the bees' stings.			_I mark_

Circle the correct answers.

1 A male bee is called a **worker**   **drone**. _I mark_

2 Pollen is a **sugary liquid**   **dusty powder**. _I mark_

3 A group of bees that lives together is called a **family**   **colony**. _I mark_

Total: ________ / 11 **marks**

😐 **Had a go** ☐   🙂 **Getting there** ☐   😄 **Got it!** ☐

Hurt No Living Thing

Hurt no living thing:
Ladybird, nor butterfly,
Nor moth with dusty wing,
Nor cricket chirping cheerily,
Nor grasshopper so light of leap,
Nor dancing gnat, nor beetle fat,
Nor harmless worms that creep.

By Christina Rossetti

Challenge 1

Read the poem to help you answer these questions.

1 What is the title of the poem?

....

1 mark

2 Who was the poem written by?

....

1 mark

3 How many lines does the poem have?

....

1 mark

4 How many animals are there in the poem?

....

1 mark

Draw lines to match each animal to its description.

1 moth   **dancing**

I mark

2 cricket   **dusty wing**

I mark

3 gnat   **fat**

I mark

4 beetle   **chirping cheerily**

I mark

Circle the word that rhymes with each word in bold.

1 thing   wing   butterfly

I mark

2 leap   cheerily   creep

I mark

3 gnat   moth   fat

I mark

Total: _______ / 11 marks

 **Had a go**    **Getting there**    **Got it!**

Junaid's Party

Junaid looked at the pile of invitation replies on the table. Everyone had said yes.

All day long, Junaid, Mum and Dad had been getting ready for the party. They'd cleaned the house and Junaid had put all his toys away. They'd blown up balloons, made sandwiches and decorated a great big birthday cake.

Junaid was excited.

It was 3 o'clock. Time for the party. Nobody came.

Then it was 4 o'clock. Still nobody came. What had gone wrong?

Junaid looked at the pile of invitations.

Oh no!

He'd told everyone the wrong time.

'Let's have a cup of tea and wait,' Mum said. 'I'm sure they'll all get here soon.'

5 o'clock came.

Ding dong! Ding dong! Ding dong! went the front doorbell.

Everyone arrived.

'You won't believe what I did,' said Junaid.

Everyone laughed.

'We'd never miss your birthday party. We love you, Junaid,' they all said.

They all ate the sandwiches and cake, and played with the balloons. It was a great party in the end.

Read the story to help you circle the correct answers.

1 Junaid's party was on **7th June**   **7th July**. `[ ]` 1 mark

2 Junaid, Mum and Dad made **chips**   **sandwiches**. `[ ]` 1 mark

3 'Let's have **a cup of tea**   **a slice of cake**,' Mum said. `[ ]` 1 mark

4 The doorbell went **Dong ding!**   **Ding dong!** `[ ]` 1 mark

1 Tick to show which things Junaid had at his party.

| invitations `[ ]` | cake `[ ]` | balloons `[ ]` |
| sandwiches `[ ]` | tea `[ ]` | toys `[ ]` |

`[ ]` 3 marks

1 Write numbers in the boxes to show the order of events in the story. One has been done for you.

Junaid, Mum and Dad had been getting ready all day long.		`[ ]` 1 mark
At 4 o'clock nobody came.		`[ ]` 1 mark
At 5 o'clock everyone arrived.		`[ ]` 1 mark
Junaid looked at the pile of invitation replies.	1	
They all ate the sandwiches and cake, and played with the balloons.		`[ ]` 1 mark
At 3 o'clock nobody came.		`[ ]` 1 mark

Total: _______ / 12 marks

😐 **Had a go** `[ ]`   🙂 **Getting there** `[ ]`   😃 **Got it!** `[ ]`

Space Science

Written by Ciaran Murtagh

Contents

Glossary

conducting carrying out

crews people who live and work together

orbit a curved path in space that goes around Earth

rocket a type of salad leaf

Index

1 Use the contents page to help you fill in the gaps in this table.

Look closely	2
Why experiment in space?	
	14
	20
Glossary and index	

1 mark

1 mark

1 mark

1 mark

Tick to show whether each statement is **True** or **False**.

		True	False
1	The book is called *Space Science*.		
2	It is written by Ciaran Murtagh.		
3	Page 12 is about being weightless.		
4	On page 18, you can find out about seeds in space.		

1 mark

1 mark

1 mark

1 mark

Answer these questions.

1 In the glossary, 'rocket' is described as a type of salad leaf. Write another meaning for the word 'rocket'. ____________

1 mark

2 Which page would you need to read to find out about

Tim Peake? ____________

1 mark

3 Which pages tell you about sleep in space? ____________

2 marks

Total: _______ / 12 marks

😐 **Had a go** ☐   🙂 **Getting there** ☐   😃 **Got it!** ☐

Mice

I think mice
Are rather nice.

Their tails are long,
Their faces small,
They haven't any
Chins at all.
Their ears are pink,
Their teeth are white,
They run about
The house at night.

They nibble things
They shouldn't touch
And no one seems
To like them much.

But I think mice
Are nice.

By Rose Fyleman

Challenge 1

Read the text to help you answer these questions.

1 What is the title of the poem?

....

1 mark

2 Who was the poem written by?

....

1 mark

3 How many lines does the poem have?

....

1 mark

4 What does the poet think about mice?

....

1 mark

Challenge 2

Write the missing words in the sentences.

1 Mice have .... tails.

2 Mice have .... faces.

3 Mice have .... ears.

4 Mice have .... teeth.

Challenge 3

Answer these questions.

1 When do mice run around the house?

....

2 Do mice have chins? ....

3 Write a word that has a similar meaning to 'nibble'.

....

4 Why do you think most people don't like mice?

....

Total: _______ / 12 marks

 **Had a go**    **Getting there**    **Got it!**

The Farmer's Boy

They walked the lane together.

The sky was dotted with stars.

They reached the rail together,

He lifted up the bars.

She neither smiled or thanked him,

Because she knew not how,

For he was only the farmer's boy

And she was the Jersey cow.

Anon.

Read the poem to help you write the missing words in the sentences.

1. They _______________ the lane together.

   1 mark

2. The sky was _______________ with stars.

   1 mark

3. They reached the _______________ together,

   1 mark

4. She neither _______________ or thanked him,

   1 mark

5. For he was only the farmer's _______________

   1 mark

6. And she was the _______________ cow.

   1 mark

Circle the correct answers.

7. The title of the poem is

   Anon   **The Farmer's Boy**.

8. The poem takes place

   at night-time   **during the day**.

9. The poem has   **9 lines**   **8 lines**.

10. The cow is a   **Jersey cow**   **Journey cow**.

Draw lines to match the rhyming words.

11. **stars**   **together**

12. **how**   **cow**

13. **together**   **bars**

1 mark

1 mark

1 mark

1 mark

1 mark

1 mark

1 mark

A World of Bears

by Adam Ursa

Contents

Index

Use the contents page to help you fill in the gaps in this table.

	Where in the world?	2
14.	North and South American bears	
15.	European bears	
16.		14
17.	Bears in danger	
18.		22

1 mark (×5)

Tick to show whether each statement is True or False.

		True	False
19.	The book is called *A World of Bears*.		
20.	The book is written by Adam Ursa.		
21.	Page 18 is about toy bears.		
22.	You can find out about what bears eat on pages 14 and 15.		

1 mark (×4)

Answer these questions.

23. Which chapter would you read to find out about teddy bears? ....

1 mark

24. Which bears can you read about in the chapter 'Bears in danger'? .... and ....

2 marks

25. Which pages tell you about bears' claws? ....

3 marks

Total: _______ / 28 marks

Email: Our Trip to London

Send

To: grandad@collins_mail.com

From: Jamie@fastweb.co.uk

Subject: Our trip to London

Dear Grandad,

We're having a great time in London.

Yesterday we went to Buckingham Palace and saw the Changing of the Guard. The soldiers looked very smart in their red uniforms and furry black hats.

This morning we went to the Houses of Parliament. We saw Big Ben. Then we walked across Westminster Bridge and took a ride on the London Eye. It was brilliant because we could see for miles and miles.

This afternoon we went on a boat trip down the River Thames. It ended at the Tower of London. I loved it there because I saw the Crown Jewels and they were the most sparkly things I have ever seen.

We'll come to see you when we get home.

Lots of love
Jamie

Challenge 1

Tick to show whether each statement is **True** or **False**.

		True	False
1	The email is from Jamie.		
2	They went to the Houses of Parliament in the afternoon.		
3	They walked across London Bridge.		
4	They saw the Crown Jewels at the Tower of London.		

1 mark

1 mark

1 mark

1 mark

Challenge 2

1. Write numbers in the boxes to put the events in the correct order. One has been done for you.

This morning we went to the Houses of Parliament.	
Then we walked across Westminster Bridge and took a ride on the London Eye.	
It ended at the Tower of London.	
This afternoon we went on a boat trip down the River Thames.	
Yesterday we went to Buckingham Palace and saw the Changing of the Guard.	1

1 mark

1 mark

1 mark

1 mark

Read the text to help you answer these questions.

1 Who did Jamie write the email to?

____

1 mark

2 What did Jamie see at Buckingham Palace?

____

1 mark

3 When did they go to the Houses of Parliament?

____

1 mark

4 What was good about being on the London Eye?

____

1 mark

5 When did Jamie go on the boat trip?

____

1 mark

6 How did Jamie describe the Crown Jewels?

____

1 mark

7 Did Jamie enjoy the trip to London? YES / NO

What makes you think this? Copy one sentence that tells you he enjoyed his trip.

____

1 mark

Total: _______ / 15 marks

EARLSWORTH CASTLE

Come and spend an action-packed day living like the ancient kings and queens of Earlsworth.

Take part in fantastic activities, including:

- Archery Academy
- Cook in the Kitchens
- Discover the Dungeons
- Juggling with Jesters
- Knight School.

Treat your family to a feast in the Royal Restaurant.

Choose from our extensive range of sandwiches, pizzas, fruit and fizzy drinks.

Entrance fee
Adults £10
Children £5
Family (2 adults, 2 children)
£25
SAT NAV: ELC 1XY

Read the text to help you answer these questions.

1 What place does the leaflet tell you about?

1 mark

2 What activities can you take part in?

5 marks

3 What can you eat in the restaurant?

3 marks

1 'Come and spend an action-packed day living like the ancient kings and queens of Earlsworth.' Circle the word below that has a similar meaning to 'ancient'.

new   **old**   **grand**   **ordinary**

1 mark

2 Find two words in the speech bubble that show the boy enjoyed the Knight School.

2 marks

3 Circle the word that suggests there is a lot to do at the castle.

fantastic   **action-packed**   **treat**   **juggling**

1 mark

Read the text to help you answer these questions.

1 Why do you think the boy loved the Knight School so much?

....

I mark

2 Why did the boy say he could hardly move in the armour?

....

I mark

3 How much does it cost for one adult and one child to visit the castle?

....

I mark

4 Which activity would you like to take part in?

....

I mark

5 Why would you like to do this activity?

....

....

I mark

Total: _______ / 18 marks

 **Had a go**   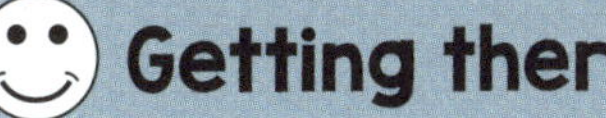 **Getting there**    **Got it!**

Animal Riddles

I am an insect.

My shiny hard shell is red like a post box

and is decorated like the dots on a dice.

Hidden beneath this armour are my delicate wings.

What am I?

I am a mollusc.

With no feet to run, I slide. Slowly.

Wherever I go, I leave a trail like shimmering silver.

My home, spiralled tightly on my back, travels with me.

What am I?

I am a mammal.

Like flames of fire, my furry coat catches the moonlight.

On my long legs I wear four black socks.

My bushy tail is topped with a white tip like fluffy candyfloss.

What am I?

I am a bird.

My eyes shine brightly like small black beads.

My beak is brightest yellow like the summer sun.

My feathers are as dark as the blackest ink.

What am I?

Answers: insect: ladybird; mollusc: snail; mammal: fox;
bird: blackbird

Tick to show the correct answers.

1. The ladybird's shell is   hard ☐   soft ☐   ☐ 1 mark

2. The top of the fox's tail is   white ☐   black ☐   ☐ 1 mark

3. The snail   runs ☐   slides ☐   ☐ 1 mark

4. The blackbird's beak is   black ☐   yellow ☐   ☐ 1 mark

Circle the correct answers.

1. 'Hidden beneath this armour are my delicate wings.' What does 'armour' suggest about the ladybird's shell?

   it is soft   **it is fluffy**   **it is hard**   ☐ 1 mark

2. 'My home, spiralled tightly on my back, travels with me.' Which of the following words has a similar meaning to 'spiral'?

   square   **circular**   **straight**   ☐ 1 mark

3. 'Like flames of fire, my furry coat catches the moonlight.' What time of day does this suggest the fox is out?

   lunchtime   **afternoon**   **night-time**   ☐ 1 mark

4. 'On my long legs I wear four black socks.' What does this tell you about the fox?

   it wears socks   **it has black legs**   **its legs are furry**   ☐ 1 mark

A simile is when one thing is compared to another thing to create a description. For example: 'My shiny hard shell is **red like a post box**.'

Copy the rest of the similes from the riddles. Clue: look for the words **like** or **as**.

1 .... 1 mark

2 .... 1 mark

3 .... 1 mark

4 .... 1 mark

5 .... 1 mark

6 .... 1 mark

7 .... 1 mark

Total: _______ / 15 marks

 **Had a go**    **Getting there**   **Got it!**

Tortoise and Hare

Early one morning, Hare was racing around the woods shouting to anyone who could hear, 'I'm the fastest animal in these woods. I'm so fast I'm like a flash of lightning. Nobody can beat me.'

Tortoise was listening nearby and slowly replied, 'I'm not so sure my friend. I think I could beat you.'

Hare started laughing. 'Whatever do you mean! Look at my strong hind legs. They're made for running, jumping and leaping. Now look at your stumpy little legs and that heavy shell you carry on your back. You couldn't beat me. Ever!'

'Well, I'm not so sure,' replied Tortoise.

And so the conversation continued all morning. By lunchtime, when the sun was high and the woods felt as hot as a baker's oven, Tortoise and Hare were ready to start their race.

All the animals had come to watch and Badger had been chosen to start the race. 'Ready, steady, go!' he shouted. Hare raced off as quick as a flash and was soon out of sight. Tortoise slowly stepped one stumpy foot in front of another.

It wasn't long until Hare reached the finish line. None of the other animals were there yet and Hare thought he'd much rather win the race with all the crowd cheering him like a hero. And so he found a nice shady spot beneath a nearby bush and settled down for a quick nap.

But whether it was because of the hot midday sun, or whether he'd worn himself out running and shouting through the woods earlier that day, Hare fell into a deep, deep sleep.

So deep that he didn't wake up until the sun began to fall below the trees and the moon began to rise. He could hear cheering. He looked up and there, slowly plodding one stumpy foot in front of the next, was Tortoise, crossing the finishing line.

The moral of the story: slow and steady wins the race.

Challenge 2

1 'They're made for running, jumping and leaping.' Circle the word below that has a similar meaning to 'leaping'.

shouting   **hiding**   **bouncing**   **running**

☐ I mark

2 'Tortoise slowly stepped one stumpy foot in front of another.' Circle the word below that has a similar meaning to 'stumpy'.

wrinkly   **long**   **light**   **short**

☐ I mark

3 'And so he found a nice shady spot beneath a nearby bush and settled down for a quick nap.' Circle the word below that has a similar meaning to 'nap'.

sleep   **play**   **sit**   **read**

☐ I mark

4 'He looked up and there, slowly plodding one stumpy foot in front of the next, was Tortoise, crossing the finishing line.' What does the word 'plodding' suggest about how Tortoise was moving? Circle the correct answer.

walking with light fast steps   **walking with slow steady steps**

☐ I mark

5 '**The moral of the story:** slow and steady wins the race.' Circle the group of words below that has a similar meaning to 'steady'.

quickly and hurriedly	even and regular	a mixture of speeds

1 mark

Challenge 3

Answer these questions about the story.

1 What time of day was it at the beginning of the story?

1 mark

2 What time of day did the race begin?

1 mark

3 Which animal started the race?

1 mark

4 Copy the words this character said to start the race.

1 mark

5 Find and copy some words that suggest Hare wanted to get the attention of the other animals at the end of the race.

1 mark

6 What time of day did the race finish?

1 mark

7 What makes you think this?

1 mark

Total: _______ / 14 marks

☺ **Had a go** ☐   ☺ **Getting there** ☐   ☺ **Got it!** ☐

Make a Fun Sock Puppet

Putting on your own puppet show is great fun. Follow these simple instructions to make your own sock puppet.

You will need:

an old sock, googly eyes, wool, a pom-pom, a piece of felt, a marker pen, a hot glue gun, scissors, an adult to help you

How to make your sock puppet:

- Put your hand inside the sock so that your thumb fits into the heel and your fingers go into the toes of the sock. This will be the mouth of your puppet.

- Cut out an oval shape from the felt. Use the hot glue gun to stick this onto the sock to make the inside of the puppet's mouth. You may find it easier to put the sock flat while you do this.

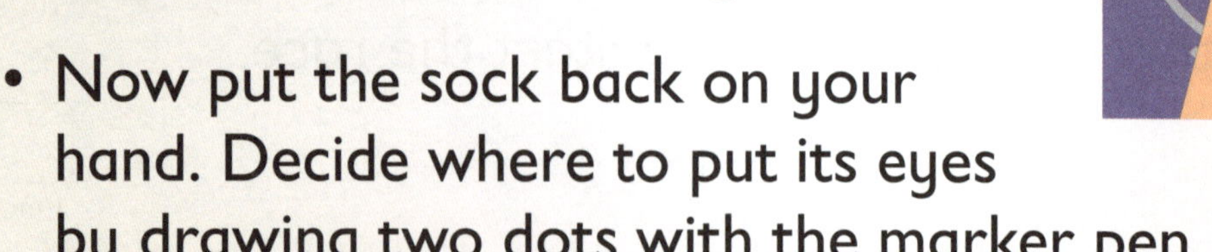

- Now put the sock back on your hand. Decide where to put its eyes by drawing two dots with the marker pen.

- Take the sock off your hand. Now use the hot glue gun to stick the googly eyes onto the dots.

- Next, cut strands of wool and glue these to the sock to make hair for your puppet.

- Finally, glue a pom-pom onto the toe end of the sock. Your puppet now has a nose.

You're now ready to put on your own puppet show.

Read the text to help you circle the correct answers.

1. What type of text is this?

    recount   **explanation**   **instructions**

    1 mark

2. Which part of the sock should you put your thumb in?

    sole   **heel**   **toe**

    1 mark

3. Which word below has a similar meaning to 'You will need'?

    method   **equipment**   **order**

    1 mark

4. Which word below has a similar meaning to 'oval'?

    square   **egg-shaped**   **triangular**

    1 mark

5. What should you use to mark the place where the eyes will go?

    scissors   **wool**   **marker pen**

    1 mark

1. Write numbers in the boxes to put the instructions in the correct order. One has been done for you.

Instruction		
Cut an oval shape from the felt.		1 mark
Cut strands of wool and glue them to the sock to make hair.		1 mark
Put your hand inside the sock.	1	
Glue a pom-pom onto the sock to make a nose.		1 mark
Decide where to put its eyes.		1 mark

Answer these questions about the text.

1. What do you use the wool for? ________________

   1 mark

2. Which two things do you need to cut with the scissors?

   ____

   2 marks

3. What is used to make the puppet's nose?

   ____

   1 mark

4. Why do the instructions suggest it would be a good idea to get an adult to help you make the sock puppet?

   ____

   1 mark

5. Which part of the sock do you put your fingers into?

   ____

   1 mark

6. Which part of the sock puppet do you use the oval felt for?

   ____

   1 mark

7. What is the pom-pom used for?

   ____

   1 mark

Total: _______ / 17 marks

 **Had a go**  **Getting there**  **Got it!** 

Four Seasons

In winter, my bare twigs
like fingers
reach toward the grey sky
grasping for light.

In spring, my branches
like arms
cradle nests of young birds
like a loving parent.

In summer, my leaves
like sparkling emeralds
hang in heavy bunches
shading picnickers below.

In autumn, my trunk
as strong as steel
stands firm as the wind
rips off my golden leaves.

Read the poem to help you tick the correct answers.

1 Who or what is the narrator of the poem?

a bird ☐   a person ☐   a tree ☐

1 mark

2 '…grasping for light.' Which of the following words has a similar meaning to 'grasping'?

grabbing ☐   breathing ☐   pushing ☐

1 mark

3 '…like sparkling emeralds…' What does the word 'emeralds' tell you about the colour of the leaves?

they are yellow ☐   they are green ☐   they are brown ☐

1 mark

4 '…rips off my golden leaves.' What does 'rips off' suggest about the wind?

it is gentle ☐   it is light ☐   it is rough ☐

1 mark

Fill in the gaps to show what each verse of the poem is about. The first one has been done for you.

winter

1 Verse 1

twigs

2 Verse 2

branches

1 mark

<table>
<tr><td>**3** **Verse 3**</td><td>...............................</td><td>1 mark</td></tr>
<tr><td></td><td>...............................</td><td>1 mark</td></tr>
<tr><td>**4** **Verse 4**</td><td>autumn ....</td><td></td></tr>
<tr><td></td><td>...............................</td><td>1 mark</td></tr>
</table>

Challenge 3

Remember, a simile is when one thing is compared to another thing to create a description. For example:

'In winter, my bare twigs

like fingers...'

Copy the rest of the similes from the poem. Clue: look for the words **like** or **as**.

1 .... 1 mark

2 .... 1 mark

3 .... 1 mark

4 .... 1 mark

Total: _______ / 12 marks

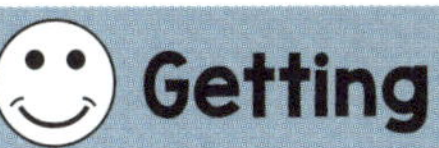

Got it!

Progress Test 2

Robert the Bruce and the Spider

Things were not going well for King Robert of Scotland. He had lost battle after battle against the English king and now he'd been forced to hide in a cave.

It was cold and damp in the cave and King Robert was feeling down in the dumps. What did he need to do to beat the English king?

One day, he noticed a spider. It was trying to build a web but kept falling down. Each time it fell, it climbed back up and tried again. Eventually, the spider's silk stuck to the cave and it was able to build its web.

King Robert thought about all the battles he'd lost and how many times the spider had tried to build its web. He knew what to do!

He left the cave and once more tried to beat the King of England in a battle. This time, he won.

The moral of the story: if at first you don't succeed, try, try and try again.

1. **Write numbers in the boxes to put these events from the story in order. One has been done for you.**

He was feeling down in the dumps.		I mark
King Robert had lost battle after battle to the English king.		I mark
He noticed a spider trying to build its web.		I mark
Eventually the spider was able to build its web.	5	I mark
King Robert beat the English king in a battle.		I mark
King Robert was hiding in a cave.		I mark

Answer these questions about the story.

2. 'He had lost battle after battle against the English king…' What is the effect of repeating the word 'battle' in this phrase?

____

1 mark

3. Find and copy a group of words that show it was uncomfortable in the cave.

____

1 mark

4. Find and copy a group of words that show Robert was unhappy.

____

1 mark

5. Write a word from the text with a similar meaning to 'defeat'. ____

1 mark

6. Which country was Robert the king of? ____

1 mark

7. Why were things going badly for King Robert at the beginning of the story?

____

1 mark

8. Who did Robert want to beat? ____

1 mark

9. Where did Robert have to hide?

____

1 mark

10. What was the spider trying to build?

____

1 mark

Marvello's Magnificent
CIRCUS
Come and join the fun at the best circus in town!
4th – 9th July
Two shows a day
Children £5   Adults £10
Families (2 adults, 2 children) £25
Coming to the Village Green
The acrobats sprung and twisted like bouncy springs. What amazing skills they have!
Mrs Begum, age 55
The trapeze artists swung like monkeys in the treetops.
J. Jones, age 7
We laughed like hyenas when the clowns came on.
S. Singh, age 6
Be astounded by our:
• Amazing acrobats
• Crazy clowns
• Marvellous magicians
• Terrific trapeze artists
New this season:
Marvello's Magnificent Circus School
Learn to tell jokes like a clown and do tricks like a magician.
Find out more by visiting our website:
www.mmcircus.com

11. The circus takes place

on the Village Green ☐   at the Town Hall. ☐   ☐

1 mark

12. There are

two shows a day ☐   three shows a day. ☐   ☐

1 mark

13. It costs

£10 for children ☐   £5 for children. ☐   ☐

1 mark

14. Mrs Begum is

45 years old ☐   55 years old. ☐   ☐

1 mark

A simile is when one thing is compared to another thing to create a description. Find and copy the similes in the text. Clue: look for the words like or as.

15. ....   ☐

1 mark

16. ....   ☐

1 mark

17. ....   ☐

1 mark

Answer these questions about the text.

18. What is the name of the circus?

....   ☐

1 mark

19. What dates does the circus take place on?

....   ☐

1 mark

20. Who gave a review of the trapeze artists?

....   ☐

1 mark

Total: _______ / 24 **marks**

The Fruit Bowl Mystery

It was another hot and sunny day at Clarendon Primary School. All the windows and doors were open to let a cooling breeze float around the school but everyone was still hot and sticky. Mrs Siddiqi picked up Class 3's fruit bowl from the shelf by the window. For the third time that week, she stopped, stared and creased her eyebrows in confusion. Where were the grapes? She was sure she'd put some in the bowl but now they were nowhere to be seen.

'Children, I think we need to have a serious talk about asking before we take, and only taking things that belong to us. This is the third time this week that the grapes have gone missing from the fruit bowl,' she said.

Playtime came. Everyone chose a piece of fruit and went out to play in the hot summer sun. Everyone gossiped about the missing fruit. Some children started to blame each other.

Some children thought it was Ravi because he was always hungry and so had probably taken the grapes to stop his tummy rumbling until playtime.

Some children thought it was Viktor because he quite often came to school without his lunch and Mrs Siddiqi had to give him some of hers.

Some children thought it was Charlie because she was new and things like this never happened before she arrived.

What was definite was that everyone started falling out or blaming someone else or crying.

Playtime finished. The children went inside and Mrs Siddiqi decided that what everyone needed was a nice story to help them cool down.

As she was reading, Mrs Siddiqi looked up. There, walking on the ledge outside the open window, was a magpie. It tipped its head to one side and looked quizzically at the empty fruit bowl. 'I wonder…' said Mrs Siddiqi to herself.

The next day, Mrs Siddiqi arranged the fruit in the fruit bowl, making sure to put a bunch of grapes on top. She opened the window and instructed the class to sit quietly and watch.

They watched and waited and then suddenly the magpie swooped down, hooked its beak around the grapes and flapped off to the playground to eat.

'Oh children, I need to apologise,' said Mrs Siddiqi. 'It wasn't any of you taking our grapes – it was that cheeky magpie.'

Everyone laughed and apologised to each other.

After that, Class 3 kept their fruit bowl away from the window. And every day they put out some grapes and bird seed for the cheeky magpie.

Challenge 1

Answer these questions about the text.

1 Where does the story take place?

....

I mark

2 Why was Mrs Siddiqi confused?

....

I mark

3 How many times had the grapes gone missing? ....

1 mark

4 Why did some children think Charlie had taken the grapes?

....

1 mark

5 How do you think the children were feeling at the end
of playtime?

....

1 mark

6 Do you think the children liked the magpie? ....

1 mark

7 What makes you think this?

....

1 mark

Answer these questions about the text.

1 What time of year do you think the story is set in?

....

1 mark

2 Find and copy the words that show Mrs Siddiqi frowned
when she was confused. ....

1 mark

3 What did Mrs Siddiqi think had happened to the grapes
at the start of the story?

....

1 mark

4 What makes you think this? ....

1 mark

5 'The children went inside and Mrs Siddiqi decided that what
everyone needed was a nice story to help them cool down.'
The children were hot after playing outside. What else could
'cool down' mean here? ....

1 mark

52

1 'All the windows and doors were open to let a cooling breeze float around the school…' Circle the word below that has a similar meaning to 'breeze'.

shower   **wind**   **fridge**   **bird**

1 mark

2 'Children, I think we need to have a serious talk about asking before we take…' Circle the word below that has a similar meaning to 'serious'.

important   **worrying**   **hilarious**   **naughty**

1 mark

3 'What was definite was that everyone started falling out or blaming someone else or crying.' Circle the word below that has a similar meaning to 'definite'.

endless   **uncertain**   **unclear**   **clear**

1 mark

4 'There, walking on the ledge outside the open window, was a magpie.' Circle the word below that has a similar meaning to 'ledge'.

sill   **pane**   **glass**   **handle**

1 mark

5 '…Mrs Siddiqi arranged the fruit in the fruit bowl, making sure to put a bunch of grapes on top.' Circle the word below that has a similar meaning to 'arranged'.

hid   **organised**   **tipped**   **protected**

1 mark

Total: _______ / 17 marks

 **Had a go**  **Getting there** 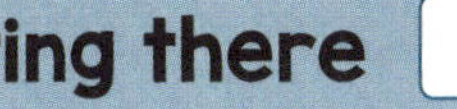 **Got it!** 

Teeth

Your teeth are important. Without them, you'd find it hard to eat your favourite food.

In your lifetime, you'll have two sets of teeth. Your baby teeth that push themselves out of your **gums** when you are still a baby. And your adult teeth that begin to appear when you are about six or seven years old.

Different types of teeth

Humans are **omnivores**. This means that we can eat plants and meat. Because of this, we have different types of teeth to help us eat these different types of food.

Incisors help us cut food.

Canines help us tear food.

Pre-molars help us crush food.

Molars help us grind food.

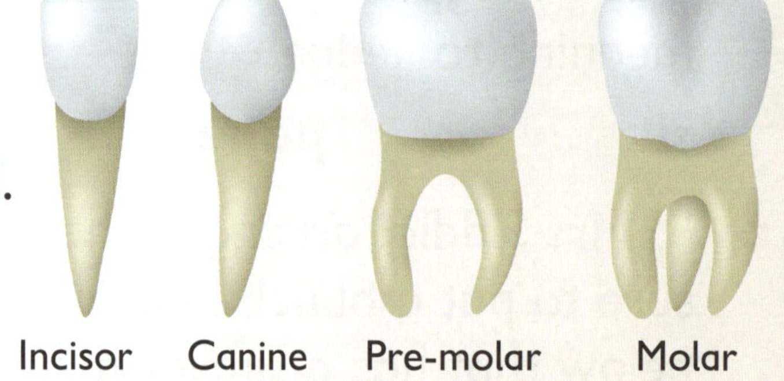

If you lose your adult teeth, you will not grow new ones, so you need to look after them carefully.

Taking care of your teeth

You should brush your teeth at least twice a day. This should take you about two minutes. You will need to brush the top and bottom teeth using gentle circular movements. You can also use **floss** to get any bits of food from between your teeth.

The surface of your teeth is covered in **enamel**. This is strong, but sugary food and drinks can damage it and cause decay. **Tooth decay** causes holes to appear in your teeth. These are called **cavities**. You can avoid cavities by brushing regularly and choosing to drink water or milk instead of sugary drinks, and eating healthy snacks such as fruit, vegetables and cheese instead of sweets.

Dentists help you look after your teeth. You should visit your dentist every six months so that they can check how healthy your teeth are.

Glossary

canines – sharp, pointed teeth

cavities – holes in your teeth

enamel – hard, shiny coating on your teeth

floss – thin, soft thread

gums – area in your mouth that teeth grow from

incisors – the teeth at the front of your mouth

molars – the large flat teeth at the back of your mouth

omnivores – animals that eat plants and meat

pre-molars – flat teeth like molars but smaller

tooth decay – damage caused to teeth by sugary food and drinks

Tick to show whether each statement about the text is **True** or **False**.

		True	False	
1	In your lifetime you will have three sets of teeth.			1 mark
2	Molars are at the back of your mouth.			1 mark
3	You should drink tea and coffee instead of sugary drinks.			1 mark
4	You should brush your teeth using circular movements.			1 mark
5	You should visit your dentist every six months.			1 mark

Draw lines to match the words with the information from the text.

1	omnivores	skin in your mouth that teeth grow from	1 mark
2	cavities	flat teeth like molars but smaller	1 mark
3	gums	sharp, pointed teeth	1 mark
4	pre-molars	holes in your teeth	1 mark
5	canines	hard, shiny coating on your teeth	1 mark
6	enamel	animals that eat plants and meat	1 mark

Answer these questions about the text.

1 How old are you when your adult teeth start to appear?

....

I mark

2 What type of teeth help us to cut food?

....

I mark

3 Where in your mouth are these teeth?

....

I mark

4 How often should you clean your teeth?

....

I mark

5 How long should you brush your teeth for?

....

I mark

6 What is the name of the thin, soft thread you can use to help clean your teeth?

....

I mark

Total: _______ / 17 marks

 **Had a go**    **Getting there**    **Got it!**

The Owl and the Pussy-Cat

The Owl and the Pussy-Cat went to sea
In a beautiful pea-green boat,
They took some honey, and plenty of money,
Wrapped up in a five-pound note.
The Owl looked up to the stars above,
And sang to a small guitar,
'O lovely Pussy! O Pussy, my love,
What a beautiful Pussy you are,
You are,
You are!
What a beautiful Pussy you are!'

Pussy said to the Owl, 'You elegant fowl!
How charmingly sweet you sing!
O let us be married! too long we have tarried:
But what shall we do for a ring?'
They sailed away, for a year and a day,
To the land where the Bong-Tree grows,
And there in a wood a Piggy-wig stood
With a ring at the end of his nose,
His nose,
His nose,
With a ring at the end of his nose.

'Dear Pig, are you willing to sell for one shilling
Your ring?' Said the Piggy, 'I will.'
So they took it away, and were married next day
By the Turkey who lives on the hill.
They dined on mince, and slices of quince,
Which they ate with a runcible spoon;
And hand in hand, on the edge of the sand,
They danced by the light of the moon,
The moon,
The moon,
They danced by the light of the moon.

By Edward Lear

1 Read the poem to find pairs of rhyming words that come **at the end of lines**. One has been done for you.

<u>boat</u> / <u>note</u>

___________ / ___________ ☐ 1 mark   ___________ / ___________ ☐ 1 mark

___________ / ___________ ☐ 1 mark   ___________ / ___________ ☐ 1 mark

___________ / ___________ ☐ 1 mark   ___________ / ___________ ☐ 1 mark

1 Write numbers in the boxes to put these lines from the poem in order. One has been done for you.

O let us be married! too long we have tarried		☐ 1 mark
The Owl and the Pussy-Cat went to sea		☐ 1 mark
They sailed away for a year and a day,		☐ 1 mark
They danced by the light of the moon.		☐ 1 mark
They dined on mince, and slices of quince,	7	
They took some honey, and plenty of money;		☐ 1 mark
The owl looked up at the stars above.		☐ 1 mark
And there in a wood a Piggy-wig stood		☐ 1 mark

Answer these questions about the poem.

1 Write down the names of all the characters in the poem.

....

4 marks

2 What colour was the boat the owl and the pussy cat sailed in?

....

1 mark

3 Which animal sang and played the guitar?

....

1 mark

4 'Dear Pig, are you willing to sell for one shilling…'
Which word in this line makes you think the poem was written a long time ago?

....

1 mark

5 What did the Owl and the Pussy-Cat want to use the ring from the Piggy-wig's nose for?

....

1 mark

6 'They dined on mince, and slices of quince…' Write the word in this line from the poem that means 'ate'.

....

1 mark

7 What did the Owl and the Pussy-Cat do at the end of the poem that shows you they were very happy?

....

1 mark

Total: _______ / 23 marks

 **Had a go**  **Getting there**  **Got it!** 

Earlsworth Castle

Earlsworth Castle is one of the finest castles in England. For over 700 years, it has been home to lords, ladies and royalty. Today it is owned by Earlsworth District Council who run it as a visitor attraction. Every year over 200,000 people visit Earlsworth, making it one of the top attractions in the country.

The Queen's Tower

The Queen's Tower was built in 1577 when Queen Elizabeth I came to visit Earlsworth. The owner at the time, Guy de Earlsworth, was so keen to impress Elizabeth that he spent over £3 million in today's money on building the tower. Elizabeth only stayed at Earlsworth for two weeks. What an expensive holiday home!

The Castle Keep

This is the original part of the castle and is less ornate than other parts of the building. This is partly due to its age (it is over 700 years old) but also its role as the castle's defensive heart. It was built for protection and security rather than for comfort and homeliness as with other parts of the castle.

The Great Hall

Built in the 14th century by Simon of Stafford, the Great Hall is famous for its fine tapestries and decorative ceiling. When you stand inside the Great Hall, it is easy to imagine eating at a grand banquet and being entertained by actors and jesters, just like the kings and queens of years gone by.

The Tudor Garden

Earlsworth's Tudor Garden is world famous. At its centre is a stunning marble fountain where visitors can throw coins and make wishes for the future. There is also an ornate aviary (bird house) which is home to Earlsworth's collection of rare finches.

Read the text to help you answer these questions.

1. Who currently owns Earlsworth Castle?

____

1 mark

2. Who was the owner of the castle when Queen Elizabeth I visited? _______________

1 mark

3. How long did Queen Elizabeth I stay at Earlsworth Castle?

____

1 mark

4. What is the name of the original part of the castle?

____

1 mark

5. Who built the Great Hall? _______________________

1 mark

6. Where would you find the marble fountain?

____

1 mark

Challenge 2

Tick to show whether each statement is **True** or **False**.

		True	False	
1	People have lived in Earlsworth Castle for over 900 years.			1 mark
2	The Queen's Tower was built in 1577.			1 mark
3	The Queen's Tower cost over £5 million pounds to build.			1 mark
4	The Keep is the oldest part of the castle.			1 mark
5	The aviary is in the Tudor Garden.			1 mark

1. 'Today it is owned by Earlsworth District Council who run it as a visitor attraction.' Circle the word below that has a similar meaning to 'attraction'.

   museum **meaning** **amusement** **enter**

   1 mark

2. 'This is the original part of the castle and is less ornate than other parts of the building.' Circle the word below that has a similar meaning to 'original'.

   silly **clever** **first** **last**

   1 mark

3. 'There is also an ornate aviary (bird house) which is home to Earlsworth's collection of rare finches.' Circle the word below that has a similar meaning to 'ornate'.

   ordinary **boring** **dull** **fancy**

   1 mark

4. '...the Great Hall is famous for its fine tapestries and decorative ceiling.' Circle the word below that has a similar meaning to 'fine'.

   impressive **intelligent** **poor** **rubbish**

   1 mark

5. '...it is easy to imagine eating at a grand banquet...' Circle the word below that has a similar meaning to 'banquet'.

   seat **feast** **table** **chair**

   1 mark

6. '...its role as the castle's defensive heart.' Circle the word below that has a similar meaning to 'defensive'.

   project **provide** **promise** **protective**

   1 mark

Total: _______ / 17 marks

😐 **Had a go** ☐   🙂 **Getting there** ☐   😃 **Got it!** ☐

Stone Soup

Long ago, there was a village where everybody had something, but nobody had a lot. The butcher had meat but no vegetables, the greengrocer had vegetables but no meat, and the people who were neither a butcher nor a greengrocer had very little at all. Nobody shared what they had, and so everybody was hungry and unhappy.

One day, a curious looking traveller arrived. He carried a large cooking pot, a small knife and a wooden ladle. He looked at the hungry, unhappy faces and began to build a fire. Next, he collected some water and poured it into the cooking pot. Then he dug deep into his jacket pocket, pulled out a small, unremarkable looking stone and dropped it into the cooking pot. 'Please join me in making some delicious stone soup,' he said.

The traveller took the wooden ladle, dipped it in the soup and said, 'Not bad. But it could do with some salt and pepper. Does anyone have any to spare?'

The villagers were so curious about the strange sounding stone soup that it didn't take long for one of the mothers to run and collect some salt and pepper, which the traveller sprinkled into the soup. The traveller thanked her, stirred the soup with the ladle and took another sip. 'Not bad. But it could do with some meat. Does anyone have any to spare?' he said.

The butcher was keen to show that he had some meat, so he quickly ran and collected some tasty chicken. The traveller chopped it up and added it to the soup. He stirred again and took another sip. 'Not bad. But it could do with some carrots. Does anyone have any to spare?' he said.

Not to be outdone by the butcher, the greengrocer ran and collected a bunch of crunchy carrots, which the traveller chopped up and added to the soup. He stirred again and took another sip and said, 'That is delicious. Please come and take a bowl.'

While the soup was being passed around, the traveller packed his possessions and slipped out of the village. The only sign he'd been there was a small, unremarkable looking stone.

Anon. adapted by Rachel Clarke

Draw a circle around the correct answer.

1 The story is set in:

a town   a village   a forest   a field

I mark

2 Where did the traveller keep the stone?

in his trouser pocket   in his jacket pocket   under his hat

I mark

3 Who had meat but no vegetables?

the greengrocer   the traveller   the butcher   the mother

I mark

4 What meat did the butcher give to the traveller?

vegetables   sausages   chicken   bread

I mark

5 Who was the first person to get ingredients for the traveller?

the greengrocer   the butcher   one of the mothers

I mark

6 What vegetables did the greengrocer give to the traveller?

carrots   potatoes   parsnips   cabbages

I mark

7 What did the traveller use to stir the soup?

a knife   a fork   a ladle   a stick

I mark

Tick to show whether each statement about the story is
True or **False**.

		True	False	
1	The traveller carried a large cooking pot, a small knife and a wooden ladle.			I mark
2	The greengrocer had meat but no vegetables.			I mark
3	Nobody shared what they had so the villagers were all hungry.			I mark
4	Water was the first ingredient added to the soup.			I mark
5	The traveller took the stone when he left the village.			I mark

Challenge 3

1 Was the soup really made from a stone?

I mark

2 Explain why you think this.

I mark

3 What do you think the moral of the story is?

I mark

4 What do you think happens next for the villagers in the story?

I mark

Total: _______ / 16 marks

😐 **Had a go** ☐   🙂 **Getting there** ☐   😃 **Got it!** ☐

Progress Test 3

Your Skeleton

Your **skeleton** is the frame of **bones** that your body is built on. It has several jobs, which include protecting your internal organs (such as your heart and lungs), giving your body a structure so that it is not floppy, and helping you to move in different directions.

When you were born, you had about 270 bones. As you've been growing, some of your bones have begun to **fuse** together. By the time your skeleton has finished growing (when you are about 21), you will have around 206 bones.

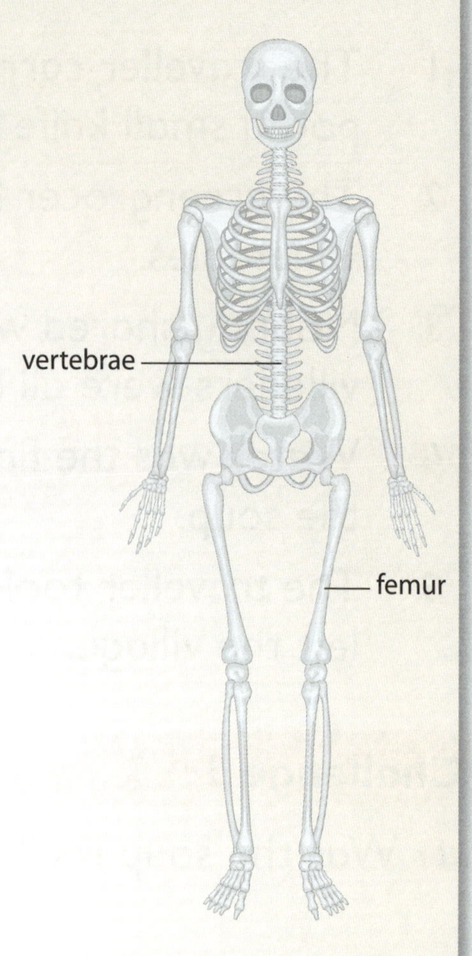

The longest bone in your body is called the **femur**. It is the long bone at the front of your thigh.

The smallest bones in your body are inside your ears. They are called the **malleus** (hammer), the **incus** (anvil) and the **stapes** (stirrup). The smallest of these, the stapes, is only 3mm wide and 2.5mm long. These tiny bones vibrate when they sense sound to help you to hear.

If you put your hands on your back, you should be able to feel bumps of bone running right down the middle. This is your **spine**. Your spine is made from 33 separate bones called **vertebrae** that all work together to help you bend and twist. These 33 little bones also hold your body upright and very importantly they protect the nerves that send messages up and down your back from your brain.

1. '...some of your bones have begun to fuse together.'
   Circle the word or words with a similar meaning to 'fuse'.

   spark   **stop growing**   **come apart**   **join**

   1 mark

2. 'These tiny bones vibrate when they sense sound to help you to hear.' Circle the word or words below with a similar meaning to 'vibrate'.

   stay still   **shake**   **make a noise**   **sing**

   1 mark

3. '...they protect the nerves that send messages up and down your back...' Circle the word or words below with a similar meaning to 'protect'.

   keep safe   **hide**   **reveal**   **keep tidy**

   1 mark

Draw lines to match information from the text.

4. **skeleton**   **the frame of bones that your body is built on**   1 mark

5. **stapes**   **hold your body upright**   1 mark

6. **vertebrae**   **the smallest bone in your body**   1 mark

Answer these questions about the text.

7. How many bones are babies born with? _______   1 mark

8. What are the bones that make up your spine called?

   _______   1 mark

9. Where in your body is your femur? _______   1 mark

Danny's Surprise

It was half-term. Mum was working so Danny was staying with Uncle Leroy. He loved staying with his mum's brother. Uncle Leroy had no children of his own so he spoiled Danny something rotten. But Danny would miss playing on his bike with his friends. He'd wanted to bring his bike but Mum said they couldn't get it there on the bus. Danny was upset but kept it to himself as he didn't want to make Mum feel bad.

On the first morning, Uncle Leroy cooked bacon and eggs for breakfast and told Danny he could watch whatever he wanted on the TV. That didn't seem too bad to Danny but he wished he could play on his bike with his friends.

'Oh, Danny. Did I tell you I've got a couple of parcels being delivered today? It's a surprise for you. Do you think you could keep an eye out for the delivery person?'

'Sure,' said Danny, settling himself into the armchair by the TV.

Time passed. Danny watched cartoons. He watched a film about living in space. He watched a program about how to recycle plastic bottles. He didn't like to think it, but he was beginning to think that Uncle Leroy wasn't as much fun as he used to be. Just then, there was a knock at the door. 'Uncle Leroy!' bellowed Danny. 'The parcels are here.'

Uncle Leroy raced through the house and opened the front door and carried the parcels inside.

'Quick Danny, come here,' he shouted. 'Look at these, they're brilliant. One for me. One for you.'

Uncle Leroy tore open the parcels. Danny watched; a huge smile beamed across his face. 'Uncle Leroy, you're the best! Can we go out on them now?'

'Definitely, but wear this helmet. Your mum would go spare if she found out you'd been riding without one.'

10. Tick to show whether each statement about the story is True or False.

	True	False
The story takes place in the summer holidays.		
Uncle Leroy is Mum's brother.		
Danny sat in an armchair to watch TV.		
Uncle Leroy opened the parcels outside.		

1 mark

1 mark

1 mark

1 mark

Answer these questions about the text.

11. Why was Danny staying with Uncle Leroy?

____

1 mark

12. Why couldn't Danny take his bike to Uncle Leroy's house?

____

1 mark

13. What do you think was in the parcels? _______________

1 mark

14. What makes you think this?

____

1 mark

Total: _______ / 17 marks

Answers

Pages 6–11 Starter Test

1. True [1]
2. False [1]
3. False [1]
4. True [1]
5. JoJo [1]
6. white [1]
7. silver [1]
8. pink [1]
9. five
10. ten
11. go
12. bite
— so [1]
— right [1]
— alive [1]
— again [1]
13. One, Two, Three, Four, Five [1]
14. eight [1]
15. a fish [1]
16. pocket [1]
17. baked [1]
18. sing [1]
19. dish [1]
20. counting [1]
21. eating [1]
22. garden [1]
23. pecked [1]
24. four and twenty / twenty-four [1]
25. the birds began to sing [1]
26. the king [1]
27. in the parlour [1]
28. hanging out the clothes [1]
29. rye
30. sing
31. money
32. clothes
— honey [1]
— pie [1]
— nose [1]
— king [1]
33. bananas, ice, milk [3]
34. blender [1]
35. bananas [1]
36. smooth [1]
37. glasses [1]
38. early [1]
39. car [1]
40. monkeys [1]
41. Saturday [1]
42. an hour [1]
43. asleep [1]

Pages 12–13

Challenge 1

1. Mum [1]
2. treat [1]
3. a tiny spot [1]
4. bought [1]

Challenge 2

1. Dad [1]
2. cake cases [1]
3. ten [1]
4. fairy cakes [1]

Challenge 3

1. butter, eggs, flour, vanilla flavouring, sugar [5]

Pages 14–15

Challenge 1

1. groups [1]
2. hive [1]
3. pour [1]

Challenge 2

1. True [1]
2. False [1]
3. False [1]
4. False [1]
5. True [1]

Challenge 3

1. drone [1]
2. dusty powder [1]
3. colony [1]

Pages 16–17

Challenge 1

1. 'Hurt No Living Thing' [1]
2. Christina Rossetti [1]
3. seven [1]
4. eight [1]

Challenge 2

1. moth
2. cricket
3. gnat
4. beetle
— dancing [1]
— dusty wing [1]
— fat [1]
— chirping cheerily [1]

Challenge 3

1. wing [1]
2. creep [1]
3. fat [1]

Challenge 1

1. 7th July [1]
2. sandwiches [1]
3. a cup of tea [1]
4. Ding dong! [1]

Challenge 2

1. cake, balloons, sandwiches [3]

Challenge 3

1.

Junaid, Mum and Dad had been getting ready all day long.	2
At 4 o'clock nobody came.	4
At 5 o'clock everyone arrived.	5
Junaid looked at the pile of invitation replies.	1
They all ate the sandwiches and cake, and played with the balloons.	6
At 3 o'clock nobody came.	3

[5]

Challenge 1

1.

Look closely	2
Why experiment in space?	4
Sleeping in space	8
Being weightless	14
The future	20
Glossary and index	21

[4]

Challenge 2

1. True [1]
2. True [1]
3. False [1]
4. True [1]

Challenge 3

1. a spaceship / a vehicle [1]
2. page 18 [1]
3. pages 6 and 8 [2]

Challenge 1

1. 'Mice' [1]
2. Rose Fyleman [1]
3. 16 [1]
4. that they are nice [1]

Challenge 2

1. long [1]
2. small [1]
3. pink [1]
4. white [1]

Challenge 3

1. at night [1]
2. No [1]
3. eat, chew, gnaw, bite etc. [1]
4. Child's own answer, e.g. because they eat things / because people think they're dirty [1]

1. walked [1]
2. dotted [1]
3. rail [1]
4. smiled [1]
5. boy [1]
6. Jersey [1]
7. The Farmer's Boy [1]
8. at night-time [1]
9. 8 lines [1]
10. Jersey cow [1]

11. stars
12. how
13. together

14. 4 [1]
15. 6 [1]
16. What's for dinner? [1]
17. 20 [1]
18. Toys and books [1]
19. True [1]
20. True [1]
21. False [1]
22. True [1]
23. Toys and books [1]
24. Pandas, Polar bears [2]
25. 5, 6, 15 [3]

Challenge 1

1. True [1]
2. False [1]
3. False [1]
4. True [1]

Challenge 2

1.

This morning we went to the Houses of Parliament.	2
Then we walked across Westminster Bridge and took a ride on the London Eye.	3
It ended at the Tower of London.	5
This afternoon we went on a boat trip down the River Thames.	4
Yesterday we went to Buckingham Palace and saw the Changing of the Guard.	1

[4]

Challenge 3

1. Grandad [1]
2. the Changing of the Guard [1]
3. This morning [1]
4. we could see for miles and miles [1]
5. This afternoon [1]
6. the most sparkly things I have ever seen [1]
7. Yes. Any one reason from: 'We're having a great time in London'; 'It was brilliant because we could see for miles and miles'; 'I loved it there.' [1]

Challenge 1

1. Earlsworth Castle [1]
2. Archery Academy, Cook in the Kitchens, Discover the Dungeons, Juggling with Jesters, Knight School [5]
3. sandwiches, pizzas, fruit [3]

Challenge 2

1. old [1]
2. loved and brilliant [2]
3. action-packed [1]

Challenge 3

1. One from: because he got to dress up in armour; because he watched the real knights put on a show [1]

2. because it was really heavy [1]
3. £15 [1]
4. Child's own choice of any activity from those listed. [1]
5. Child's own answer that explains their reason. [1]

Challenge 1

1. hard [1]
2. white [1]
3. slides [1]
4. yellow [1]

Challenge 2

1. it is hard [1]
2. circular [1]
3. night-time [1]
4. it has black legs [1]

Challenge 3

1. decorated like the dots on a dice [1]
2. a trail like shimmering silver [1]
3. Like flames of fire, my furry coat [1]
4. a white tip like fluffy candyfloss [1]
5. eyes shine brightly like small black beads [1]
6. brightest yellow like the summer sun [1]
7. as dark as the blackest ink [1]

Challenge 1

1. as hot as a baker's oven [1]
2. as quick as a flash [1]

Challenge 2

1. bouncing [1]
2. short [1]
3. sleep [1]
4. walking with slow steady steps [1]
5. even and regular [1]

Challenge 3

1. early morning [1]
2. lunchtime [1]
3. Badger [1]
4. Ready, steady, go! [1]

5. he'd much rather win the race with all the crowd cheering him like a hero [1]

6. evening / night-time [1]

7. the sun was going down / the moon was coming up [1]

Pages 40–42

Challenge 1

1. instructions [1]
2. heel [1]
3. equipment [1]
4. egg-shaped [1]
5. marker pen [1]

Challenge 2

Cut an oval shape from the felt.	2
Cut strands of wool and glue them to the sock to make hair.	4
Put your hand inside the sock.	1
Glue a pom-pom onto the sock to make a nose.	5
Decide where to put its eyes.	3	**[4]**

Challenge 3

1. to make the hair [1]
2. felt and wool [2]
3. a pom-pom [1]
4. because the glue is hot / the hot glue gun could burn you and you also have to use scissors [1]
5. the toe
6. its mouth
7. To make the puppet's nose.

Pages 43–45

Challenge 1

1. a tree [1]
2. grabbing [1]
3. they are green [1]
4. it is rough [1]

Challenge 2

1. spring [1]
2. summer [1]
3. leaves [1]
4. trunk [1]

Challenge 3

1. branches like arms [1]
2. cradle nests of young birds like a loving parent [1]

3. leaves like sparkling emeralds [1]
4. trunk as strong as steel [1]

Pages 46–49 Progress Test 2

1.

He was feeling down in the dumps.	3
King Robert had lost battle after battle to the English king.	1
He noticed a spider trying to build its web.	4
Eventually the spider was able to build its web.	5
King Robert beat the English king in a battle.	6
King Robert was hiding in a cave.	2	**[5]**

2. It shows that Robert had lost many battles. [1]
3. It was cold and damp in the cave. [1]
4. down in the dumps [1]
5. beat [1]
6. Scotland [1]
7. he kept losing battles [1]
8. the King of England [1]
9. in a cave [1]
10. a web [1]
11. on the Village Green [1]
12. two shows a day [1]
13. £5 for children [1]
14. 55 years old [1]
15. The trapeze artists swung like monkeys in the treetops. [1]
16. We laughed like hyenas when the clowns came on. [1]
17. The acrobats sprung and twisted like bouncy springs. [1]
18. Marvello's Magnificent Circus [1]
19. 4th – 9th July [1]
20. J. Jones [1]

Challenge 1

1. Clarendon Primary School / in a classroom **[1]**

2. because the grapes had gone missing / she was sure she'd put grapes in the fruit bowl but they weren't there **[1]**

3. three times **[1]**

4. because she was new and things like that hadn't happened before **[1]**

5. unhappy / sad / anxious / angry **[1]**

6. Yes **[1]**

7. They put food out for it. **[1]**

Challenge 2

1. summer **[1]**

2. creased her eyebrows **[1]**

3. one of the children had taken them **[1]**

4. One from: she wanted to have a serious talk about only taking their own things; she apologised later in the story **[1]**

5. the children needed to cool their tempers / everyone was cross **[1]**

Challenge 3

1. wind **[1]**

2. important **[1]**

3. clear **[1]**

4. sill **[1]**

5. organised **[1]**

Challenge 1

1. False **[1]**

2. True **[1]**

3. False **[1]**

4. True **[1]**

5. True **[1]**

Challenge 2

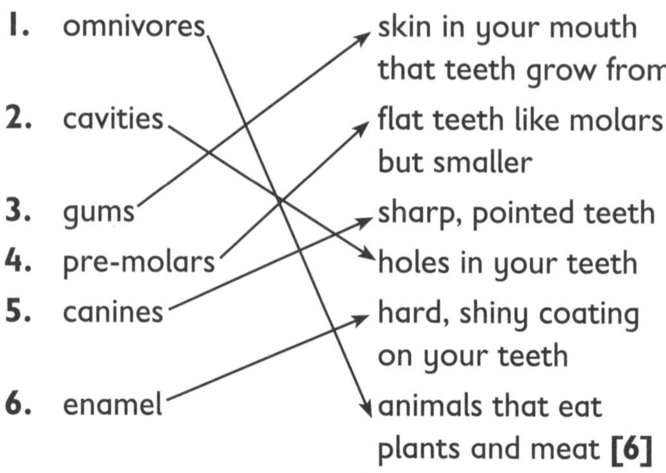

Challenge 3

1. six or seven years old **[1]**

2. incisors **[1]**

3. at the front **[1]**

4. at least twice a day **[1]**

5. about two minutes **[1]**

6. floss **[1]**

Challenge 1

1. above / love; guitar / are; sing / ring grows / nose; will/ hill; spoon/ moon **[6]**

Challenge 2

O let us be married! too long we have tarried	4
The Owl and the Pussy-Cat went to sea	1
They sailed away for a year and a day,	5
They danced by the light of the moon.	8
They dined on mince, and slices of quince,	7
They took some honey, and plenty of money;	2
The owl looked up at the stars above.	3
And there in a wood a Piggy-wig stood	6 **[5]**

Challenge 3

1. Owl, Pussy-Cat, Piggy-wig, Turkey [4]
2. green / pea-green [1]
3. Owl [1]
4. shilling [1]
5. a wedding ring [1]
6. dined [1]
7. danced (hand in hand) [1]

Challenge 1

1. Earlsworth District Council [1]
2. Guy de Earlsworth [1]
3. two weeks [1]
4. The Keep [1]
5. Simon of Stafford [1]
6. in the Tudor Garden [1]

Challenge 2

1. False [1]
2. True [1]
3. False [1]
4. True [1]
5. True [1]

Challenge 3

1. amusement [1]
2. first [1]
3. fancy [1]
4. impressive [1]
5. feast [1]
6. protective [1]

Challenge 1

1. a village [1]
2. in his jacket pocket [1]
3. the butcher [1]
4. chicken [1]
5. one of the mothers [1]

6. carrots [1]
7. a ladle [1]

Challenge 2

1. True [1]
2. False [1]
3. True [1]
4. True [1]
5. False [1]

Challenge 3

1. No [1]
2. It added no flavour; the soup was made from the other ingredients [1]
3. It's good to share what you have. [1]
4. One from: they carry on using the stone; they learn to share what they have [1]

1. join [1]
2. shake [1]
3. keep safe [1]
4. skeleton ⟶ the frame of bones that your body is built on [1]
5. stapes ⟶ hold your body upright [1]
6. vertebrae ⟶ the smallest bone in your body [1]
7. about 270 [1]
8. vertebrae [1]
9. thigh / leg [1]
10. False, True, True, False [4]
11. because it was half-term and Mum was working [1]
12. because they couldn't take it on the bus [1]
13. bikes [1]
14. because Uncle Leroy said Danny needed to wear a helmet to go riding / Danny says, 'Can we go out on them now?' [1]

Fill in your score for each progress test in the window of the rocket.

Progress
Test 1
Progress
Test 2
Progress
Test 3